STATE REPORTS

South Central

ARKANSAS ★ KANSAS ★ LOUISIANA ★ MISSOURI ★ OKLAHOMA

By
Thomas G. Aylesworth
Virginia L. Aylesworth

CHELSEA HOUSE PUBLISHERS
New York   Philadelphia

Produced by James Charlton Associates
New York, New York.

Copyright © 1992 by Chelsea House Publishers, a division of Main Line Book Co.

First Printing

1   3   5   7   9   8   6   4   2

Library of Congress Cataloging-in-Publication Data

Aylesworth, Thomas G.
    South Central: Arkansas, Kansas, Louisiana, Missouri, Oklahoma/by
Thomas G. Aylesworth, Virginia L. Aylesworth.
    p. cm. — (State reports)
    Includes bibliographical references and index.
    Summary: Discusses the geographical, historical, and cultural aspects of
Louisiana, Arkansas, Missouri, Kansas, and Oklahoma.
    ISBN 0-7910-1047-3
        0-7910-1394-4 (pbk.)
    1. Southwestern States—Juvenile literature. [1. Southern States.] I. Aylesworth, Virginia L.
II. Title. III. Series: Aylesworth, Thomas G. State reports.

F396.A95   1991   90-28835
976—dc20   CIP
                                             AC

Contents

Arkansas

State Seal, **5**; State Flag and Motto, **7**; State Capital, **9**; State Name and Nicknames, **9**; State Flower, Tree, Bird, Beverage, Gem, Insect, Mineral, Musical Instrument, Rock, and Song, **10**; Population, **10**; Geography and Climate, **10**; Industries, **11**; Agriculture, **11**; Government, **11**; History, **11**; Sports, **12**; Major Cities, **12**; Places to Visit, **13**; Events, **13**; Famous People, **14**; Colleges and Universities, **14**; Where To Get More Information, **14**.

Kansas

State Seal, **15**; State Flag, Banner, and Motto, **17**; State Capital, **18**; State Name and Nicknames, **20**; State Flower, Tree, Bird, Animal, Insect, Song, and March, **20**; Population, **20**; Geography and Climate, **20**; Industries, **21**; Agriculture, **21**; Government, **21**; History, **21**; Sports, **23**; Major Cities, **23**; Places to Visit, **23**; Events, **24**; Famous People, **25**; Colleges and Universities, **26**; Where To Get More Information, **26**.

Louisiana

State Seal, **27**; State Flag and Motto, **29**; State Capital, **31**; State Name and Nicknames, **31**; State Flower, Tree, Bird, Crustacean, Dog, Drink, Fossil, Fruit, Gem, Insect, Reptile, and Songs, **32**; Population, **33**; Geography and Climate, **33**; Industries, **33**; Agriculture, **33**; Government, **33**; History, **34**; Sports, **34**; Major Cities, **35**; Places to Visit, **36**; Events, **36**; Famous People, **37**; Colleges and Universities, **38**; Where To Get More Information, **38**.

Missouri

State Seal, **39;** State Flag and Motto, **41;** State Capital, **43;** State Name and Nicknames, **43;** State Flower, Tree, Bird, Mineral, Rock, Fossil, Insect, Musical Instrument, Tree Nut, and Song, **44;** Population, **44;** Geography and Climate, **44;** Industries, **45;** Agriculture, **45;** Government, **45;** History, **45;** Sports, **46;** Major Cities, **46;** Places to Visit, **47;** Events, **48;** Famous People, **48;** Colleges and Universities, **50;** Where To Get More Information, **50.**

Oklahoma

State Seal, **51;** State Flag and Salute to the Flag, **53;** State Capital, **54;** State Name and Nicknames, **54;** State Flower, Tree, Bird, Animal, Colors, Fish, Grass, Poem, Reptile, Rock, and Songs, **56;** Population, **56;** Geography and Climate, **57;** Industries, **57;** Agriculture, **57;** Government, **57;** History, **57;** Sports, **58;** Major Cities, **59;** Places to Visit, **59;** Events, **60;** Famous People, **60;** Colleges and Universities, **61;** Where To Get More Information, **61.**

Bibliography 62

Index 63

Arkansas

The state seal of Arkansas, adopted in 1864, is circular. At the bottom is a shield bearing pictures of a steamboat, plow and beehive, and a sheaf of wheat. These stand for the state's industry and agriculture. To the left of the shield is the Angel of Mercy holding a banner on which is printed "Mercy," and to the right is the sword of justice bearing the word "Justice." Behind the shield is an American eagle carrying a banner inscribed with the state motto. Above the eagle is the Goddess of Liberty surrounded by thirteen stars. Around the circle is printed "Great Seal of the State of Arkansas."

State Flag

The state flag was adopted in 1913 and amended in 1923. A large white diamond, symbolizing Arkansas' status as the only diamond-producing state, is surrounded by 25 stars on a blue border inside a field of red. Inside the diamond is inscribed "Arkansas" and four stars, standing for the four nations whose flags have flown over Arkansas—France, Spain, the Confederate States of America, and the United States of America.

State Motto

Regnat Populus

This motto, Latin for "The people rule," was adopted in 1907.

Hikers enjoy the scenery of the Buffalo National River, where private citizens live and farm in the valley under an agreement with the National Park Service.

The state capitol building in Little Rock has been used as a stand-in for the U.S. Capitol in Washington in several films.

State Capital

Little Rock has always been the capital city. The present capitol building was begun in 1899 but was not completed until 1916. Modeled after the U.S. Capitol, this edifice is made of Batesville marble and Indiana Bedford limestone, and cost $2.5 million.

State Name and Nicknames

The name Arkansas was first recorded by Father Jacques Marquette in 1673. He took it from the Kansa Indians, who used it to mean "downstream people."

The official nickname of the state is the *Land of Opportunity*. It has also been referred to as the *Bowie State*, after the famous knife made for Jim Bowie. Another nickname is the *Hot Water State* because of the hot springs that can be found there.

State Flower

In 1901, Arkansas selected the apple blossom, *Pyrus malus,* as the state flower.

State Tree

The pine, *Pinus palustris,* was named state tree of Arkansas in 1939.

State Bird

The State Federation of Women's Clubs convinced the state legislature to select the mockingbird, *Mimus polyglottos,* as state bird in 1929.

State Beverage

Milk was named state beverage in 1985.

State Gem

The diamond was adopted state gem in 1967.

State Insect

The honeybee, *Apis mellifera,* became the state insect in 1973.

State Mineral

Adopted in 1967, the state mineral is the quartz crystal.

The apple blossom is the state flower.

State Musical Instrument

The fiddle has been the state musical instrument since 1985.

State Rock

Bauxite, an aluminum ore, was designated state rock in 1967.

State Song

Adopted by the legislature in 1917, the state song is "Arkansas," by Eva Ware Barnett.

Population

The population of Arkansas in 1990 was 2,362,239, making it the 33rd most populous state. There are 44.4 people per square mile—51.5 percent of the population live in towns and cities. More than 99 percent of the people of Arkansas were born in the United States.

Geography and Climate

Bounded on the north by Missouri; on the east by Missouri, Tennessee, and Mississippi; on the south by Louisiana and Texas; and on the west by Texas and Oklahoma, Arkansas has an area of 53,187 square miles, making it the 27th largest state. The climate consists of long, hot summers and mild winters. Rain is plentiful.

In the eastern part of the state are deltas and prairies; in the south are lowlands and in the northwest are highlands. The highest point in the state, at 2,753 feet, is atop Magazine Mountain. The lowest, at 55 feet, is along the Ouachita River. The major waterways of the state are the Mississippi, Arkansas, Ouachita, St. Francis, Red,

The waterfalls in the Ozark National Forest.

and White rivers. The largest lake is Lake Chicot.

Industries

The principal industries of Arkansas are agriculture, tourism, and forestry. The chief manufactured products are lumber, paper, food products, home appliances, chemicals, electric motors, furniture, garments, machinery, auto and airplane parts, and petroleum products.

Agriculture

The chief crops of the state are soybeans, rice, cotton, watermelons, wine grapes, blueberries, and apples. Arkansas is also a livestock state, and there are estimated to be some 1.75 million cattle, 540,000 hogs and pigs, and $1.65 billion worth of poultry on its farms. Oak, hickory, gum, cypress, and pine trees are harvested. Abrasives, bauxite, and bromine are important mineral resources. Commercial fishing brings in some $7.3 million per year.

Government

The governor of Arkansas is elected to a four-year term, as are the lieutenant governor, secretary of state, attorney general, treasurer, auditor, and land commissioner. The state legislature, or general assembly, which meets in odd-numbered years, consists of a 35-member senate and a 100-member house of representatives. Senators are elected by senatorial districts and serve four-year terms. Representatives are elected from representative districts and serve two-year terms. The most recent state constitution was adopted in 1874. In addition to its two U.S. senators, Arkansas has four representatives in the House of Representatives. The state has six votes in the electoral college.

History

Before the Europeans arrived, what was to become Arkansas was inhabited by three principal tribes of Indians—the Caddo, Osage, and Quapaw. The Spanish explorer Hernando de Soto crossed into the territory in 1541. Father Jacques Marquette and Louis Jolliet traveled down the Mississippi to the mouth of the Arkansas River in 1673. In 1682, Robert Cavelier, Sieur de la Salle, claimed the lands of the Mississippi Valley for France, naming it Louisiana after King Louis XIV. In 1686, the first permanent settlement in the area, Arkansas Post, was established.

Spain took over the region in 1763 after a series of wars, but in 1800 it was returned to France. After the Louisiana Purchase of 1803, the area became a territory of the United States. In 1812, Arkansas became a part of the Missouri Territory. Fort Smith was built in 1817 to protect the settlers from Indian attacks. The Arkansas Territory, which also included a part of Oklahoma, was created in 1819, and in 1836, Arkansas became the 25th state in the Union.

Even though Arkansas was a slave state, a state convention voted to remain in the Union when the other southern states seceded in 1861. Later that year, when President Lincoln called for troops, the convention met again and voted to secede. In 1862, the Union Army forced Confederate troops into southern Arkansas after the Battle of Pea Ridge. Little Rock was captured in 1863, and in 1864, Arkansas had a Union capital in Little Rock and a Confederate capital in Washington. After the war, Arkansas was occupied by Union troops until 1874. It was readmitted to the Union in 1868.

The economy expanded in the late 1800s as railroads were built and farming and industry prospered. Bauxite mines opened in 1887, and later, large sawmills were built. In the 1900s, rice and soybean farms were started, and in 1921, oil was discovered near El Dorado. World War II brought further expansion, as farming and mining prospered. Today, Arkansas continues to enjoy economic and agricultural progress.

Sports

Arkansas is a sports state, especially when it comes to football. The University of Arkansas has won many post-season bowls including the Orange Bowl, the Sugar Bowl, and the Cotton Bowl.

Major Cities

Fort Smith (population 71,626). The town grew up around the fort, which was built in 1817. By 1842, the town had a population of nearly 500. It became a supply center for gold-rush wagons heading for California in 1848. A lawless town, it was not cleaned up until 1875. Today it is a leading manufacturing city, home to more than 200 industrial plants.

Things to see in Fort Smith: Fort Smith National Historic Site, Old Fort Museum, Fort Smith Art Center, and Fort Chaffee.

Little Rock (population 180,450). Settled in 1812, the capital city is the center for transportation, education, culture, and government. Its name came from French explorers, who called this site on the Arkansas River "La Petite Roche."

> *Things to see in Little Rock:* State Capitol, Old State House, Arkansas Territorial Restoration, Arkansas Museum of Science and History, Decorative Arts Museum, Old Mill (1828), and Little Rock Zoo.

Pine Bluff (population 56,636). Founded in 1819, Pine Bluff was occupied by Union troops in 1863 and remained in Union hands until the end of the Civil War. Today it is an industrial city surrounded by vast recreation areas.

> *Things to see in Pine Bluff:* Jefferson County Historical Museum, and Dexter Harding House.

Places to Visit

The National Park Service maintains eight areas in the state of Arkansas: Arkansas Post National Memorial, Buffalo National River, Fort Smith National Historic Site, Hot Springs National Park, Pea Ridge National Military Park, Ouachita National Forest, Ozark National Forest, and St. Francis National Forest. In addition, there are 28 state recreation areas.

Berryville: Cosmic Cavern. The cavern is Arkansas' largest underground lake.

Bull Shoals Lake: Mountain Village 1890. An Ozark village with authentic buildings, including a bank and general store.

Hot Springs: Tiny Town. This is an indoor mechanical village.

Mountain View: Ozark Folk Center State Park. Fifty old buildings are located in this 915-acre site.

Events

There are many events and organizations that schedule activities of various kinds in the state of Arkansas. Here are some of them.

Sports: National Explorer Canoe Race (Batesville), Arkansas All Arabian Horse Show (Little Rock), Riverboat Days and State Catfish Cooking Contest (Newport), World Championship Duck Calling Contest (Stuttgart).

Arts and Crafts: Festival of the Two Rivers (Arkadelphia),

The skyline of Little Rock, which got its name from a small rock outcropping that served as an Arkansas River landmark since 1722.

Jonquil Festival (Hope).

Music: Ozark Folk Festival (Eureka Springs), Warfield Concert Series (Helena), Arkansas Symphony (Little Rock), Arkansas Folk Festival (Mountain View), Arkansas State Fiddler's Contest (Mountain View), Gospel Festival (Springdale).

Entertainment: Arkansas-Oklahoma State Fair (Fort Smith), Water Festival (Greers Ferry Lake), Ozark Frontier Trail Festival (Heber Springs), Riverfest (Little Rock), Arkansas State Fair and Livestock Show (Little Rock), Tontitown Grape Festival (Springdale).

Tours: Spring Tour of Historic Homes (Eureka Springs), Walking Tour (Hot Springs).

Theater: Arkansas Repertory Theatre (Little Rock), Ozark Mountain Music (Rogers).

Famous People

Many famous people were born in the state of Arkansas. Here are a few:

Lou Brock b. 1939, El Dorado. Hall of Fame baseball player

Helen Gurley Brown b. 1922, Green Forest. Magazine editor

Glen Campbell b. 1936, Billstown. Country singer

Johnny Cash b. 1932, Kingsland. Country singer

Dizzy Dean 1911-74, Lucas. Hall of Fame baseball pitcher

George E. Haynes 1880-1960, Pine Bluff. Civil rights leader

Alan Ladd 1913-64, Hot Springs. Film actor: *The Great Gatsby, Shane*

Laurence Luckinbill b. 1934, Fort Smith. Film actor: *The Boys in the Band, Such Good Friends*

Douglas MacArthur 1880-1964, Little Rock. World War II and Korean War general

John McClellan 1896-1977, Sheridan. Senate leader

Dick Powell 1904-63, Mountain View. Film actor: *It Happened Tomorrow, Susan Slept Here*

Third baseman Brooks Robinson won twelve Gold Glove awards for the Baltimore Orioles.

Charlie Rich b. 1932, Forest City. Country singer

Brooks Robinson b. 1937, Little Rock. Hall of Fame baseball player

Colleges and Universities

There are many colleges and universities in Arkansas. Here are the more prominent, with their locations, dates of founding, and enrollments.

Arkansas State University, State University, 1909, 9,181

University of Arkansas, Fayetteville, 1871, 14,281; Little Rock, 1927, 10,842; Monticello, 1909, 1,978; Pine Bluff, 1873, 3,077

Where To Get More Information

Arkansas Department of Parks and Tourism
1 Capitol Mall
Little Rock, AR 72201
Or Call 1-800-643-8383

Kansas

The state seal of Kansas, adopted in 1861, is circular. In the center is a country scene in which the sun is rising over some hills. There is a river with a steamboat, a settler's cabin, an ox train and wagon, and a herd of buffalo being chased by two Indians. In the foreground is a man plowing the soil. The state motto appears over the picture, and around the circle is printed "Great Seal of the State of Kansas" and "January 29, 1861"—the date of Kansas' entry into the Union.

State Flag

The state flag, adopted in 1927 and amended in 1961, has the state seal in the center on a blue background. Below the seal is the word "Kansas," and above it is a sunflower.

State Banner

The state banner of Kansas, approved in 1925, is solid blue and has a sunflower in the center.

State Motto

Ad Astra per Aspera

This Latin motto can be translated as "To the stars through difficulties." It was adopted in 1861.

The green hills of Gypsum offer a contrast to the yellow prairie land that covers the central section of Kansas.

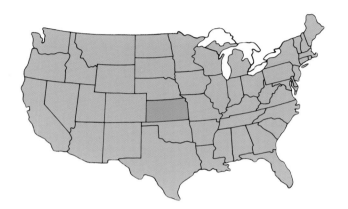

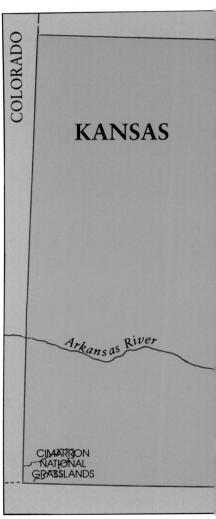

State Capital

   Topeka has been the capital of Kansas since its entry into the Union in 1861. The capitol building was first used in 1870 and was finally completed in 1903 at a cost of about $3.2 million. On the dome is a statue of Ceres, the Roman goddess of crops.

The state capitol building, an example of Classic Revival architecture, is in Topeka.

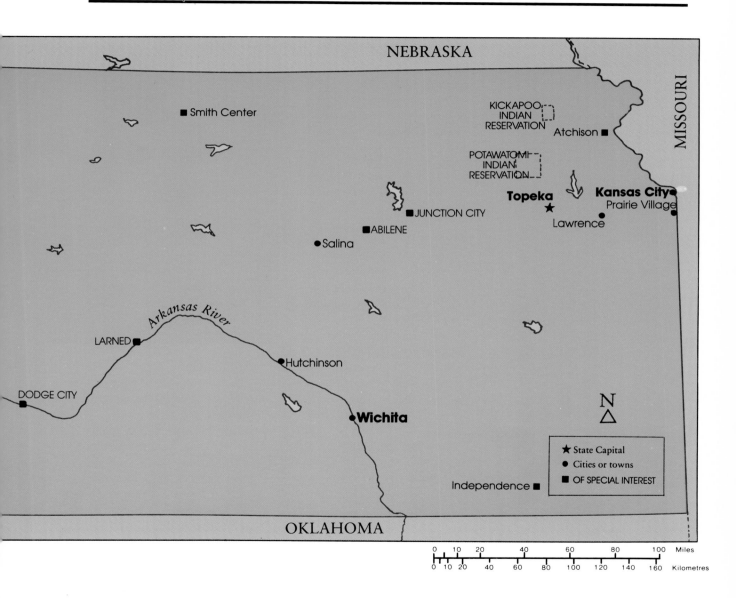

NEBRASKA

MISSOURI

■ Smith Center

KICKAPOO
INDIAN
RESERVATION

Atchison ■

POTAWATOMI
INDIAN
RESERVATION

Topeka
★

JUNCTION CITY

Kansas City
Prairie Village

■ ABILENE

Lawrence

● Salina

Arkansas River

LARNED ■

Hutchinson

DODGE CITY ■

Wichita

N
△

★ State Capital
● Cities or towns
■ OF SPECIAL INTEREST

Independence ■

OKLAHOMA

| 0 | 10 | 20 | | 40 | | 60 | | 80 | | 100 | Miles |

| 0 | 10 | 20 | 40 | | 60 | | 80 | | 100 | | 120 | | 140 | | 160 | Kilometres |

State Name and Nicknames

The name Kansas comes from *Kanze*, which meant "south wind" in the Kansa Indian language.

Most commonly, Kansas is known as the *Sunflower State*, after the state flower. It has also been called *Bleeding Kansas* because of the fighting that occurred there before the Civil War. Other nicknames are the *Squatter State* (because of the squatters who settled there) and the *Jayhawker State* (after the pillagers who first occupied the territory).

The sunflower is the state flower.

State Flower

The sunflower, *Helianthus annuus,* was named the state flower of Kansas in 1903.

State Tree

The cottonwood, *Populus deltoides,* has been the state tree since 1937.

State Bird

School children voted the western meadowlark, *Sturnella neglecta,* to be the state bird, and it was adopted in 1937.

State Animal

In 1955, the American buffalo, *Bison americanus,* was selected as the state animal.

State Insect

Named in 1976, the honeybee, *Apis mellifera,* is the state insect.

State Song

"Home on the Range," with words by Dr. Brewster Higley and music by Dan Kelly, was adopted as state song in 1947.

The western meadowlark is the state bird.

State March

In 1935, Kansas designated "The Kansas March," by Duff E. Middleton, as state march.

Population

The population of Kansas in 1990 was 2,485,600, making it the 32nd most populous state. There are 30.2 persons per square mile—66.7 percent of the population live in towns and cities.

Geography and Climate

Bounded on the north by Nebraska, on the east by Missouri, on the south by Oklahoma, and on the west by Colorado, Kansas has as area of 82,277 square miles, making it the 14th largest state. The climate is temperate, with great extremes in temperature between summer and winter.

In the east are hilly plains, in the central section are prairies, and in the west are high plains. The highest point in the state, at 4,039 feet, is atop Mount Sunflower in Wallace County. The lowest point, at 679 feet, is in Montgomery County. The major waterways in Kansas are the Kansas, Arkansas, Missouri, Big Blue, Cimarron, Neosho, Republican, Saline, Solomon, Smoky Hill, and Verdigris rivers. The largest lake in the state is Milford Lake.

Industries

The principal industries of Kansas are agriculture, machinery, mining, and aerospace. The chief manufactured products are processed foods, aircraft, petroleum products, and farm machinery.

Agriculture

The chief crops of the state are wheat, sorghum, corn, and hay. Kansas is also a livestock state, and there are estimated to be some 5.86 million cattle, 1.45 million hogs and pigs, 277,000 sheep, and 2.1 million chickens and turkeys on its farms. Oak and walnut trees are harvested. Cement, salt, and crushed stone are important mineral resources.

Government

The governor of Kansas is elected to a four-year term, as are the lieutenant governor, secretary of state, attorney general, treasurer, and commissioner of insurance. The state legislature, which meets annually, has a 40-member senate and a 125-member house of representatives. Senators serve four-year terms and representatives serve two-year terms. Each legislator is elected from a separate district. The most recent state constitution was adopted in 1859. In addition to its two U.S. senators, Kansas has four representatives in the U.S. House of Representatives. The state has six votes in the electoral college.

History

Before the Europeans arrived, what was to become Kansas was inhabited by Kansa (or Kaw), Osage, Pawnee, and Wichita Indians in the east, and Arapaho, Cheyenne, Comanche, Kiowa, and other tribes in the west. The first Europeans to visit the area were the Spanish explorer Francisco

Kansas is known for its sweeping fields of wheat, one of the state's most important crops.

Vásquez de Coronado and his men, who were looking for gold in 1541. They found no treasure and left without establishing any settlements.

French fur trappers came into the region in the early 1700s, but they, too, did not settle there. Most of Kansas was part of the Louisiana Territory when France sold it to the United States in 1803.

A small section in the southwestern part of Kansas belonged to Spain, and it later became a part of Mexico, and then part of Texas. Kansas became part of the District of Louisiana, the Louisiana Territory, and the Missouri Territory.

In 1827, the first permanent settlement, Fort Leavenworth, was established. In the 1850s, Kansas became the symbol of a nationwide struggle. Kansas became a territory in 1854 when the region was opened for settlement. Almost immediately arguments over whether it should be a free state or a slave state began. Violence broke out, people were killed, and towns were burned. Kansas became the 34th state of the Union in 1861, after several southern states had seceded.

During the Civil War, Kansas sent a higher proportion of its men to fight than any other state. Several southern raids occurred in the state, and Lawrence was burned in 1863. In the 1860s and 1870s, with the arrival of the railroads, agriculture became a big business. Many towns became cattle settlements. Coal, lead, and zinc were mined in Kansas in the early 1900s. Helium was discovered in 1903 near Dexter, and oil was discovered near El Dorado in 1915.

Lawrence was the site of much bloodshed between proslavery forces, who wanted Kansas to be a slave state, and antislavery supporters, who fought to keep it free.

During World War I, Kansas produced war supplies, and farm production was increased. During the Great Depression of the 1930s, farms and factories failed. But World War II brought another boom. Army camps were built or expanded and Kansas became one of the centers of aircraft manufacturing. Today, Kansas is an extremely important farm and factory state.

Sports

Kansas has long been a sports-minded state. The University of Kansas has won the NCAA championship in basketball (1952, 1988), and Wichita State University has won the NCAA baseball championship (1989).

Major Cities

Kansas City (population 161,087). Settled in 1843, Kansas City is a manufacturing town, as evidenced by the presence of grain elevators, steel mills, automobile manufacturers, soap factories, railway yards, and other industries.

Things to see in Kansas City: Huron Indian Cemetery, Wyandotte County Historical Society and Museum, Agricultural Hall of Fame and National Center, Old Shawnee Town, and Community Nature Center Nature Trail.

Topeka (population 115,266). Founded in 1854, the capital city began as a terminus of the Atchison, Topeka and Santa Fe railroad. Today it is a manufacturing center and the home of the Menninger Foundation, the famous psychiatric clinic and research center.

Things to see in Topeka: State Capitol, Governor's Mansion, Kansas State Historical Society, Kansas Museum of History, Ward-Meade Historical Home, Gage Park, Topeka Zoo, and Potwin Place.

Wichita (population 279,272). Settled in 1868, Wichita is best known for the manufacture of private aircraft. Originally, Wichita was an Indian trading post,

Memorial Stadium is packed with spectators for a Saturday afternoon college football game at the University of Kansas.

and became a cow capital in the 1870s.

Things to see in Wichita: Century II, Wichita-Sedgwick County Historical Museum, Indian Center Museum, Omnisphere and Science Center, Wichita Art Museum, Wichita Art Association, Old Cowtown Museum, Sedgwick County Zoo and Botanical Garden, Clifton Square, Fellow-Reeve Museum of History and Science, Edwin A. Ulrich Museum of Art, and Lake Afton Public Observatory.

Places to Visit

The National Park Service maintains three areas in the state of Kansas: Fort Larned National Historic Site, Fort Scott National Historic Site, and Cimarron National Grasslands. In addition, there

Bell Hall is a college for military officers in Fort Leavenworth, the oldest permanent military post west of the Missouri River.

are 22 state recreation areas.

Abilene: Eisenhower Center. The Eisenhower family home contains original furnishings.

Atchison: International Forest of Friendship. A concrete path winds its way through the forest, which contains trees from 50 states and 33 countries.

Concordia: Brown Grand Opera House. This restored 1907 theater is in Renaissance style.

Council Grove: Pioneer Jail. Built in 1849, this was the only jail on the Santa Fe Trail.

Dodge City: Historic Front Street. This is a reconstruction of two blocks of the frontier town of the 1870s.

Hiawatha: Iowa, Sac and Fox Presbyterian Mission Museum. Built in 1837, this was one of the earliest Indian missions west of the Missouri River.

Independence: "Little House on the Prairie." This is a reproduction of Laura Ingalls Wilder's family home.

Leavenworth: Fort Leavenworth. The working fort also contains a museum of pioneer history and the Army of the West.

Liberal: Coronado Museum. This museum contains historical artifacts and Dorothy's house from *The Wizard of Oz*.

Marysville: Pony Express Barn Museum. Exhibits from the Pony Express days.

Medicine Lodge: Medicine Lodge Stockade. This is a replica of an 1874 stockade.

Norton: Station 15. This is a replica of an 1859 stagecoach depot.

Phillipsburg: Old Fort Bissell. Replicas of an Indian fort and sod house, a log cabin and schoolhouse.

Seneca: Fort Markley and Indian Village. This old western town contains a Victorian home, museum and art gallery.

Smith Center: Home on the Range Cabin. The restored cabin where Dr. Brewster Higley wrote the words for "Home on the Range."

Events

There are many events and organizations that schedule activities of various kinds in the state of Kansas. Here are some of them.

Sports: National Greyhound Meet (Abilene), Central Kansas Free Fair and PRCA Wild Bill Hickock Rodeo (Abilene), Inter-State Fair and Rodeo (Coffeyville), North Central Kansas Rodeo (Concordia), Rodeo (Hays), National Junior College Basketball Tournament (Hutchinson), Kansas Relays (Lawrence), International Pancake Race (Liberal), Riley

County Fair and Kaw Valley Rodeo (Manhattan), McPherson County Fair and Rodeo (McPherson), Virgil Herron Rodeo (Parsons), Rodeo (Phillipsburg), Tri-Rivers Fair and Rodeo (Salina), Huff 'n Puff Balloon Rally (Topeka), National Championship Baseball Tournament (Wichita).

Arts and Crafts: River Valley Art Festival (Arkansas City), Twin Rivers Festival (Emporia), Historic Preservation Association Antique Show and Flea Market (Fort Scott), Fine Arts Festival (Goodland), International Holiday Festival (Wichita).

Music: Bell Tower (Lawrence), Messiah Festival (Lindsborg), Bell Tower (Manhattan), Arts in the Park (Manhattan), Wichita Symphony Orchestra (Wichita), Jazz Festival (Wichita), Wichita River Festival (Wichita), Bluegrass Festival (Winfield).

Entertainment: Arkalalah Celebration (Arkansas City), Atchison County Fair (Atchison), Mexican Fiesta (Chanute), Fall Festival (Chanute), Dodge City Days (Dodge City), Long Branch Saloon (Dodge City), Good Ol' Days Celebration (Fort Scott), Pioneer Harvest Fiesta (Fort Scott), Beef Empire Days (Garden City), Mexican Fiesta (Garden City), Great Bend Frontier Festival (Great Bend),

Halloween Parade (Hiawatha), Kansas State Fair (Hutchinson), Renaissance Festival (Kansas City), Buffalo Bill Cody Days (Leavenworth), Five-State Free Fair (Liberal), Mid-Summer's Day Festival (Lindsborg), St. Lucia Festival (Lindsborg), Indian Summer Days (Medicine Lodge), Bethel College Fall Festival (Newton), Mini-Sapa Days (Oberlin), John Brown Jamboree (Osawatomie), Smoky Hill River Festival (Salina), Steam Engine and Antique Farm Engine Show (Salina), Combat Air Museum Airshow and Superbatics (Topeka), Indian Powwow (Wichita), Octoberfest (Wichita), Christmas Through the Windows at Old Cowtown Museum (Wichita), Cowley County Fair (Winfield).

Theater: Brown Grand Opera House (Concordia), Summer Theater (Emporia), Broadway R.F.D. (Lindsborg).

Famous People

Many famous people were born in the state of Kansas. Here are a few:

Gwendolyn Brooks b. 1917, Topeka. Pulitzer Prize-winning poet: *Annie Allen, The Bean Eaters*

Walter P. Chrysler 1875-1940,

Wamego. Automobile executive

Amelia Earhart 1897-1937, Atchison. Record-setting aviator

Dennis Hopper b. 1936, Dodge City. Film actor: *Easy Rider, Hoosiers*

William Inge 1913-73, Independence. Pulitzer Prize-winning novelist and playwright: *Picnic, The Dark at the Top of the Stairs*

Walter Johnson 1887-1946, Humboldt. Hall of Fame baseball pitcher

Buster Keaton 1896-1966, Piqua. Film actor: *The General, Limelight*

Emmett Kelly 1898-1979, Sedan. Circus clown

Stan Kenton 1912-79, Wichita. Band leader and pianist

Edgar Lee Masters 1869-1950, Garnett. Poet: *Spoon River Anthology, The New Spoon River*

Charlie "Bird" Parker 1920-55, Kansas City. Jazz saxophonist

Damon Runyon 1880-1946, Manhattan. Short story writer: *Guys and Dolls, Money From Home*

Jim Ryun b. 1947, Wichita. Champion runner

Gale Sayers b. 1943, Wichita. Hall of Fame football player

Earl W. Sutherland 1915-74, Burlingame. Nobel Prize-winning biochemist

John Cameron Swayze b. 1906, Wichita. Television newsman

Lyle Waggoner b. 1935, Kansas City. Television actor: *The Carol Burnett Show, Wonder Woman*

William Allen White 1868-1944, Emporia. Newspaper editor

Colleges and Universities
There are many colleges and universities in Kansas. Here

Edgar Lee Masters practiced law for twenty-five years before the publication of Spoon River Anthology.

are the more prominent, with their locations, dates of founding, and enrollments.

Emporia State University, Emporia, 1863, 6,021

Fort Hays State University, Hays, 1902, 4,997

Friends University, Wichita, 1898, 1,287

Kansas State University of Agriculture and Applied Science, Manhattan, 1863, 20,110

Pittsburg State University, Pittsburg, 1903, 5,960

Saint Mary of the Plains College, Dodge City, 1952, 1,003

University of Kansas, Lawrence, 1863, 26,320

Washburn University of Topeka, Topeka, 1865, 6,574

Wichita State University, Wichita, 1892, 17,419

Where To Get More Information
The Travel and Tourism Division, Department of Commerce
400 West 8th Street, 5th Floor
Topeka, KS 66603-3957
Or Call 1-800-2KANSAS

Louisiana

The state seal of Louisiana, adopted in 1902, is circular. In the center is a picture of a female pelican protecting her three offspring. Above the pelican is "Union and Justice," and beneath is "Confidence." Around the edge of the seal is "State of Louisiana."

State Flag

The state flag, adopted in 1912, bears the drawing from the state seal on a blue background. Beneath it is a white banner with the state motto.

State Motto

Union, Justice and Confidence
The motto was adopted in 1864. Previously, the motto had been *Justice, Union and Confidence.*

The day comes to a close in Louisiana, where the sunset stretches over bayou country.

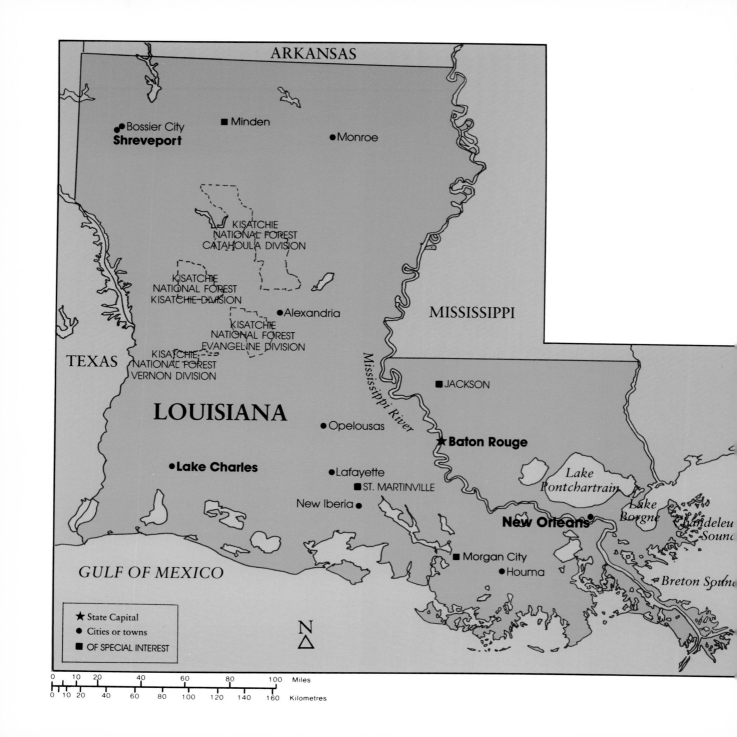

The state capitol building in Baton Rouge was built in 1932 by Huey P. Long, a former Louisiana governor.

State Capital

The first capital of Louisiana was New Orleans (1812-30). Then came Donaldsonville (1830-31), New Orleans again (1831-49), Baton Rouge (1849-62), and New Orleans yet again (1862-82). Finally, Baton Rouge became the capital again, and has remained so ever since. The capitol building is located on 27 acres of parklike grounds. Completed in 1932 at a cost of $5 million, it is a 34-story edifice in the Art Moderne school of American architecture.

State Name and Nicknames

Robert Cavelier, Sieur de la Salle, claimed the Mississippi Valley for France in 1682, naming it La Louisianne for King Louis XIV of France.

Louisiana has several nicknames, but the most common one is the *Pelican State,* after the state bird. *Bayou State* refers to the number of bayous, and the *Fisherman's Paradise* refers to the excellent fishing waters in the state. It has also been called the *Child of the Mississippi* because of its geological origin, and the *Sugar State* because of the importance of that crop.

State Flower
  The magnolia, *Magnolia grandiflora,* was named the state flower in 1900.

State Tree
  The bald cypress, *Taxodium distichum,* was adopted as the state tree in 1963.

State Bird
  The eastern brown pelican, *Pelecanus occidentalis,* became the state bird in 1966. Previously, the pelican, with no specific type mentioned, had been the state bird.

The magnolia is the state flower.

State Crustacean
  The crawfish (or crayfish—family *Astacidae*) has been the state crustacean since 1983.

State Dog
  In 1979, the Louisiana Catahoula leopard dog was adopted as state dog.

State Drink
  Milk was made the state drink in 1983.

State Fossil
  In 1976, petrified palmwood was adopted as state fossil.

State Fruit
  In 1980, the state legislature passed an act making a different fruit the state fruit each year: peach (1980), watermelon (1981), fig (1982), strawberry (1983), peach (1984), orange (1985), tomato (1986), cantaloupe (1987).

State Gem
  The agate has been the state gem since 1976.

The eastern brown pelican is the state bird.

State Insect
  The honeybee, *Apis mellifera,* became the state insect in 1977.

State Reptile
  The alligator, *Alligator mississippiensis,* was adopted as state reptile in 1983.

State Songs
  Louisiana has two state songs, "Give Me Louisiana," by Doralice Fontane, and "You Are My Sunshine," by Jimmie H. Davis and Charles Mitchell.

Population

The population of Louisiana in 1990 was 4,238,216, making it the 21st most populous state. There are 88.8 persons per square mile—68.7 of the population live in towns and cities.

Geography and Climate

Bounded on the north by Arkansas and Mississippi, on the east by Mississippi and the Gulf of Mexico, on the south by the Gulf of Mexico, and on the west by Texas, Louisiana has an area of 47,752 square miles, making it the 31st largest state. The climate is subtropical.

There are lowlands and marshes along the Mississippi River and the Red River Valley, and upland hills elsewhere. The highest point in the state, at 535 feet, is atop Driskill Mountain. The lowest point, at 5 feet below sea level, is in New Orleans. The major waterways of the state are the Mississippi, Atchafalaya, Red, Black, Calcasieu, Ouachita, Pearl, and Sabine rivers. The largest lake is Lake Pontchartrain.

Industries

The principal industries of Louisiana are trade, construction, transportation, and mining. The chief manufactured products are chemical products, foods, transportation equipment, electronic equipment, apparel, and petroleum products.

Agriculture

The chief crops of the state are soybean, sugarcane, rice, corn, cotton, sweet potatoes, melons, and pecans. Louisiana is also a livestock state, and there are estimated to be some 573,000 cattle,

Sugarcane is one of Louisiana's most important crops.

154,000 hogs and pigs, 21,000 sheep, and 600,000 poultry on its farms. Pine, hardwood, and oak trees are harvested. Salt, sand, gravel, and sulphur are important mineral resources. Commercial fishing brings in about $264.2 million each year.

Government

The governor of Louisiana is elected to a four-year term, as are the lieutenant governor, secretary of state, attorney general, treasurer, commissioner of agriculture, and superintendent of education. The state legislature, which meets annually, consists of a 39-member senate and a 105-member house of representatives. Senators and representatives serve four-year terms, and are elected from 39 senatorial districts and 105 representative districts. The most recent state constitution was adopted in 1974. In addition to its two U.S. senators, Louisiana has seven representatives in the House of Representatives. The state has nine votes in the electoral college.

History

Before the Europeans arrived in what was to become Louisiana, the area was populated by about 30 Indian tribes. Among them were the Atakapa, Caddo, Chitimacha, and the Tunica. The first European to visit the territory was the Spanish explorer Hernando de Soto in 1541. He was looking for gold; after his death, in 1542, his men left the region.

The French explorer Robert Cavelier, Sieur de la Salle, arrived in 1682 with 50 men. He claimed the entire Mississippi Valley for France, naming it Louisiana for King Louis XIV. In 1699, Louisiana became a French royal colony. In 1712, the King gave trading rights to Antoine Crozat, and the area became a proprietary colony. The first permanent settlement in the region was Natchitoches, established in

1714. In 1718, the governor, Jean Baptiste Le Moyne, began building New Orleans.

In 1731, Louisiana again became a royal colony, but in 1762, France turned most of it over to the Spanish. During the Revolutionary War, New Orleans was used as a port by the American forces. In 1803, Spain returned Louisiana to France. As a result of the Louisiana Purchase of 1803, Louisiana became part of the United States and was renamed the Territory of Orleans. In 1812, Louisiana became the 18th state in the Union.

During the War of 1812, the British tried to capture New Orleans. They were defeated by Andrew Jackson, who repelled them in the Battle of New Orleans. After the war, the area's shipping industry boomed. The state joined the Confederacy prior to the Civil War. In 1862, Mississippi River forts were bombarded and New Orleans was occupied by Union forces. Louisiana remained under

military rule until it was readmitted to the Union in 1868.

By 1883, railroads had moved into the state and the mouth of the Mississippi had been deepened to accommodate ocean-going ships. In the early 1900s, oil was discovered near Jennings and White Castle, and natural gas was found near Monroe.

During World War II, industry expanded. Today, Louisiana is a state that looks to the past while planning for the future.

Sports

Louisiana is a sports state, especially in football. Every year the Sugar Bowl is held in New Orleans. It has been won by Tulane (1935) and Louisiana State University (1959, 1965, 1968). In addition, LSU has won the Cotton Bowl (1963, 1966) and Orange Bowl (1944, 1962).

On the professional level, the New Orleans Saints of the National Football League play in the Superdome.

Major Cities

Baton Rouge (population 219,419). Founded in 1719, the capital city was settled by the French. Today it is a major Mississippi River port and an industrial center. The city has beautiful antebellum mansions and gardens.

Things to see in Baton Rouge: Oakley (1799), State Capitol, Governor's Mansion, Louisiana Arts and Science Center, Old Governor's Mansion, Laurens Henry Cohn Sr. Memorial Plant Arboretum, Greater Baton Rouge Zoo, Magnolia Mound Plantation, Mount Hope Plantation, Rural Life Museum, USS *Kidd*, Heritage Museum and Village, Parlange Plantation (1750), Nottoway Plantation (1859), and Glynnwood Plantation Home.

New Orleans (population 557,927). Founded in 1718, the state's largest city is cosmopolitan, with an old-world charm in its French Quarter. It is also one of the busiest ports in the United States.

Things to see in New Orleans: Jackson Square, Jackson

The muddy waters of the Mississippi River run through the city of Baton Rouge.

Brewery, Cabildo (1795), Pirate's Alley, St. Louis Cathedral (1794), Presbytère (1791), French Market, Old U.S. Mint, Madame John's Legacy (1727), Adelina Patti's House and Courtyard, Court of Two Sisters, Historic New Orleans Collection, Old Absinthe House, Louis Armstrong Park, Preservation Hall, Levee and docks, Barataria Unit, New Orleans Museum of Art, Dueling Oaks, Garden District, Audubon Park and Zoological Gardens, World

Trade Center of New Orleans, Pharmacy Museum (1823), Confederate Museum, and St. Charles Avenue Streetcar.

Shreveport (population 205,820). Founded in 1839, Shreveport was originally a thriving river town. Now it is a heavily industrialized city and a lumber-producing center.

Things to see in Shreveport: Louisiana State Exhibit Museum, Veteran's Park, C. Bickham Dickson Park, R. S.

Barnwell Memorial Garden and Art Center, R. W. Norton Art Gallery, American Rose Center, and Water Town.

Places to Visit

The National Park Service maintains two areas in the state of Louisiana: Jean Lafitte National Historical Park and Preserve, and Kisatchie National Forest. In addition, there are 14 state recreation areas.

Alexandria: Kent House. Built in 1800, this is a restored French Colonial plantation.

Franklin: Arlington Plantation. This Greek Revival mansion, built in 1840, stands on the banks of the Bayou Teche.

Jackson: Asphodel Plantation. Built from 1820 to 1830, this antebellum mansion accepts overnight guests.

Lafayette: Acadian Village: A Museum of Acadian Heritage and Culture. This restored bayou town contains houses, a general store, and a chapel.

Lake Charles: "Charpentier" Historical District. Victorian homes are located in 40 square blocks of downtown.

Many: Hodges Gardens. Wild and cultivated flowers cover 4,700 acres.

Minden: Germantown Museum. Three buildings, built in 1835 by German settlers, contain records and artifacts of the original inhabitants.

Morgan City: Swamp Gardens and Wildlife Zoo. This outdoor swamp museum depicts the history of the Atchafalaya Basin.

Natchitoches: Fort St. Jean Baptiste State Commemorative Area. This replica of the 1732 fort includes a barracks, chapel, and Indian huts.

New Iberia: Shadows-on-the-Teche. Built in 1834, this is a Classical Revival home.

Opelousas: Jim Bowie Museum. This museum contains Bowie memorabilia.

Events

There are many events and organizations that schedule activities of various kinds in the state of Louisiana. Here are some of them.

Sports: Super Derby Festival (Bossier City), Southwest Fat Stock Show and Rodeo (Lake Charles), Contraband Days (Lake Charles), Sugar Bowl

The French Quarter, with the elaborate ironwork on its buildings and exciting nightlife on its streets, is the cultural center of New Orleans.

College Football Classic (New Orleans).

Arts and Crafts: FestForAll (Baton Rouge), Fall Crafts Festival (Baton Rouge), Lagniappe on the Bayou (Houma), Azalea Trail (Lafayette), Red River Revel Arts Festival (Shreveport).

Music: River City Blues Festival (Baton Rouge), Cajun Country Outdoor Opry and Fais Do Do (Houma), New Orleans Opera Association (New Orleans), New Orleans Symphony (New Orleans), New Orleans Jazz and Heritage Festival (New Orleans).

Entertainment: North Louisiana Cotton Festival and Fair (Bastrop), International Acadian Festival (Baton Rouge), Greater Baton Rouge State Fair (Baton Rouge), Taste of the Bayou (Houma), Blessing of the Shrimp Fleet (Houma), International Rice Festival (Lafayette), Battle of Pleasant Hill Reenactment (Many), Sawmill Days (Many), Sabine Free State Festival (Many), Louisiana Shrimp and Petroleum Festival and Fair (Morgan City), Natchitoches-Northwestern Folk Festival (Natchitoches), Christmas Festival of Lights (Natchitoches), Sugarcane Festival and Fair (New Iberia), Mardi Gras (New Orleans), French Quarter Festival (New

Orleans), Spring Fiesta (New Orleans), Louisiana Yambilee (Opelousas), Louisiana Peach Festival (Ruston), Festa Italiana (Shreveport), Louisiana State Fair (Shreveport), Christmas in Roseland (Shreveport).

Tours: Annie Miller's Swamp and Marsh Tours (Houma), Natchitoches Pilgrimage (Natchitoches), Historic Washington Annual Pilgrimage (Opelousas), Audubon Pilgrimage (St. Francisville).

Theater: Louisiana Passion Play (Calhoun), Festival International de Louisiane (Lafayette), Le Petit Theatre du Vieux Carré (New Orleans), Saenger Performing Arts Center (New Orleans).

Famous People

Many famous people were born in the state of Louisiana. Here are a few:

Louis "Satchmo" Armstrong 1900-71, New Orleans. Jazz trumpeter

Pierre G. T. Beauregard 1818-93, near New Orleans. Confederate general

Terry Bradshaw b. 1948, Shreveport. Hall of Fame football player

Truman Capote 1924-84,

New Orleans. Author: *In Cold Blood, Breakfast at Tiffany's*

Van Cliburn b. 1934, Shreveport. Concert pianist

Michael DeBakey b. 1908, Lake Charles. Heart transplant surgeon

Fats Domino b. 1928, New Orleans. Singer

Bryant Gumbel b. 1948, New Orleans. Television host

Elvin Hayes b. 1945, Rayville.

Terry Bradshaw spent his career as quarterback for the Pittsburgh Steelers.

Hall of Fame basketball player

Lillian Hellman 1905-84, New Orleans. Dramatist: *Watch on the Rhine, The Little Foxes*

Al Hirt b. 1922, New Orleans. Jazz trumpeter

Mahalia Jackson 1911-72, New Orleans. Gospel singer

Dorothy Lamour b. 1914, New Orleans. Film actress: *The Hurricane, Road to Singapore*

Jerry Lee Lewis b. 1935, Ferriday. Rock singer

King Oliver 1885-1938, near New Orleans. Jazz cornetist

Mel Ott 1909-58, Gretna. Hall of Fame baseball player

Willis Reed b. 1942, Hico. Hall of Fame basketball player

Bill Russell b. 1934, Monroe. Hall of Fame basketball player

Edward D. White 1845-1921, Lafourche Parish. Chief Justice of the Supreme Court

Andrew Young b. 1932, New Orleans. Ambassador to the United Nations

Colleges and Universities

There are many colleges and universities in Louisiana. Here are the more prominent, with their locations, dates of founding, and enrollments.

Centenary College of Louisiana, Shreveport, 1825, 1,033

Louisiana State University and A & M College, Baton Rouge, 1860, 25,977

Louisiana State University in Shreveport, 1965, 4,110

Louisiana Tech University, Ruston, 1894, 10,018

Loyola University, New Orleans, 1849, 4,916

McNeese State University, Lake Charles, 1939, 7,579

Northeast Louisiana University, Monroe, 1931, 10,560

Northwestern State University of Louisiana, Natchitoches, 1884, 6,925

Southeastern Louisiana University, Hammond, 1925, 9,551

Southern University and A & M College, Baton Rouge, 1880, 9,811

Tulane University of Louisiana, New Orleans, 1834, 11,516

University of Southwestern Louisiana, Lafayette, 1898, 15,515

Xavier University of Louisiana, New Orleans, 1925, 2,906

Where To Get More Information

Department of Culture, Recreation and Tourism
Louisiana Office of Tourism
P.O. Box 94291
Baton Rouge, LA 70804-9291
Or Call 1-800-33-GUMBO

Missouri

The state seal of Missouri dates back to 1822. It is circular. In the center is a small circle with a bear and crescent on the left and the arms of the United States on the right. Around the circle is printed "United We Stand, Divided We Fall." The circle is flanked on each side by a grizzly bear. Underneath is a banner with the state motto and the date "MDCCCXX" (1820—the year of the first constitution). Atop the circle is a helmet, and above that are 24 stars, showing that Missouri was the 24th state in the Union. Around the seal is printed "Great Seal of the State of Missouri."

State Flag

The state flag, adopted in 1913, has three horizontal stripes: red, white, and blue. In the center is the state seal surrounded by a blue ring containing 24 white stars.

State Motto

Salus Populi Suprema Lex Esto

This Latin motto, adopted in 1822, means "The welfare of the people shall be the supreme Law."

Big Spring is a scenic area near Van Buren.

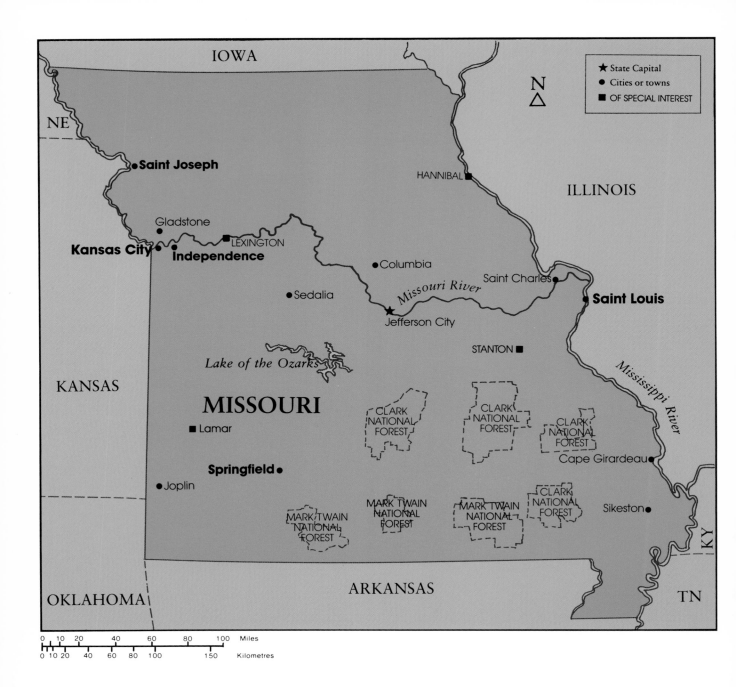

The capitol building in Jefferson City, where a statue of Thomas Jefferson greets visitors at the entryway.

State Capital

St. Charles was the capital of Missouri from 1821 (when it became a state) until 1826, when Jefferson City was selected. The present capitol building was completed in 1918 at a cost of $4,215,000. It is a Renaissance-Classical building made of Burlington limestone. A statue of Ceres, the Roman goddess of crops, is atop the dome.

State Name and Nicknames

The state was named for the Missouri River, which, in turn, was named for the Missouri Indians.

The most common nickname for Missouri is the *Show Me State,* which denotes stubbornness accompanied by common sense.

State Flower

Adopted in 1923, the state flower is the red haw, wild haw, or hawthorn blossom, *Crataegus*.

State Tree

The flowering dogwood, *Cornus florida*, was named the state tree in 1955.

State Bird

The bluebird, *Sialia sialis*, has been the state bird since 1927.

State Mineral

In 1967, galena, an ore of lead, was selected as the state mineral.

State Rock

Mozarkite was named the state rock in 1967.

State Fossil

The crinoid, or sea lily, was designated state fossil in 1989. It is related to the starfish.

State Insect

The honeybee, *Apis mellifera*, was selected as the official state insect in 1985.

The hawthorn blossom is the state flower.

State Musical Instrument

In 1987, the fiddle was chosen state musical instrument.

State Tree Nut

The Eastern Black Walnut, *juglans nigra*, was chosen official tree nut of Missouri in 1990.

State Song

"Missouri Waltz," with music by John Valentine Eppel and words by J. R. Shannon, was adopted as state song in 1949.

Population

The population of Missouri in 1990 was 5,137,804, making it the 15th most populous state. There are 73.7 persons per square mile—68.1 percent of the population live in towns and cities. More than 98 percent of the people of Missouri were born in the United States.

Geography and Climate

Bounded on the east by Illinois, Kentucky, and Tennessee; on the south by Arkansas; on the west by Oklahoma, Kansas, and Nebraska; and on the north

The bluebird is the state bird.

by Iowa; Missouri has an area of 69,697 square miles, making it the 19th largest state. The climate is continental, and is influenced by Canadian, Gulf, and southwestern air.

In the north there are hills, plains, and prairies. The south is rough and hilly. In the southeast are plains, and in the west is low country. The highest point in the state, at 1,772 feet, is atop Taum Sauk Mountain in Iron County. The lowest point, at 230 feet, is along the St. Francis River in Dunklin County. The major waterways in Missouri are the Mississippi, Missouri, Current, Black, James, St. Francis, Gasconade, Little Piney, Meramec, and White rivers. The largest lake in the state is Lake of the Ozarks, which is man-made.

Industries

The principal industries of the state of Missouri are agriculture, tourism, and aerospace. The chief manufactured products are transportation equipment, food products, electrical and electronic equipment, and chemicals.

Agriculture

The chief crops of the state are soybeans, corn, wheat, and cotton. Missouri is also a livestock state, and there are estimated to be some 4.5 million cattle, 2.9 million hogs and pigs, 125,000 sheep, 7.9 million chickens, and 16.5 million turkeys on its farms. Oak and hickory trees are harvested. Crushed stone, limestone, lead, zinc, and copper are important mineral resources.

Government

The governor of Missouri is elected to a four-year term, as are the lieutenant governor, secretary of state, state treasurer, attorney general, and state auditor. The state legislature, or general assembly, which meets annually, consists of a senate of 34 members and a house of representatives of 163 members. Senators, who serve four-year terms, are elected from 34 senatorial districts, and representatives, who serve two-year terms, are elected from 163 representative districts. The most recent state constitution was adopted in 1945. In addition to its two U.S. senators, Missouri has nine representatives in the U.S. House of Representatives. The state has 11 votes in the electoral college.

History

Before the Europeans arrived, what was to become Missouri

Saint Joseph is the home of the Stetson Hat Company.

was inhabited by prehistoric Indians known as Mound Builders. These were later followed by the Osage, Fox, and Sauk Indians. The French explorers Father Jacques Marquette and Louis Jolliet may have been the first Europeans to visit the area when they discovered the mouth of the Missouri River in 1673. In 1682, the entire Mississippi Valley was claimed for France by Robert Cavelier, Sieur de la Salle, who named it Louisiana, after the French king Louis XIV.

French trappers, traders, and miners moved into the territory, and the first settlement was founded near present-day St. Louis around 1700. This mission was abandoned three years later, and the first permanent settlement was founded at Ste. Genevieve around 1735. France gave Spain the region in 1762, but Spain was forced to return it in 1800. After the Louisiana Purchase of 1803, Missouri became part of the United States in the territory of Upper Louisiana.

The Missouri Territory was organized in 1812. During the War of 1812, the British armed the Indians and urged them to attack the Missouri settlers. These raids ended in 1815, when a peace treaty was signed between the Indians and the U.S. government. Many of the settlers were sympathetic to the slave states and petitioned Congress to be admitted to the Union as a slave state. The admission occurred in 1821, and Missouri became the 24th state.

A Missouri state convention voted to stay in the Union at the outbreak of the Civil War, but when President Lincoln called for troops, Governor Claiborne F. Jackson refused. This caused a battle between Union soldiers and Missouri militiamen at Boonville in 1861. The state convention met again, and threw out the pro-South state leaders. After the war, St. Louis and Kansas City became important transportation centers, and the fur trade became less important.

During World War I and II, Missouri's mining, manufacturing, and agriculture expanded to supply the demands of the armed forces. Today, Missouri is a leader in industry, farming, mining, and culture.

Sports

Missouri has always been a sports-minded state. On the professional level, the St. Louis Cardinals of the National League play baseball in Busch Stadium and the Kansas City Royals of the American League play in Royals Stadium. In football, the Kansas City Chiefs of the National Football League play in Arrowhead Stadium. The St. Louis Blues of the National Hockey League play in the St. Louis Arena.

Major Cities

Jefferson City (population 33,619). Settled around 1823, Jefferson City was selected as the state capital in 1821, when it contained only a foundry, shop, and mission. Today, "Jeff City" is a prosperous small town whose chief activity is government.

Things to see in Jefferson City: State Capitol, Missouri State Museum, Missouri Veterinary Medical Foundation Museum.

Kansas City (population 448,159). Settled in 1838, Kansas City was once a trading post. It became a boom town when the railroads arrived. Today it is a city with broad streets and beautiful parks.

Things to see in Kansas City: Kansas City Museum, Liberty Memorial Museum, Toy and Miniature Museum, Nelson-Atkins Museum of Art, Antiques and Art Center, Kansas City Art Institute (1885), City Market, Kaleidoscope, Union Cemetery (1857), Kansas City Zoo, Benjamin Ranch, Van Ackeren Gallery, and Jesse James Bank Museum.

St. Louis (population 453,085). Settled in 1764, St. Louis was originally a fur-trading post. In 1804, it was the site of the official transfer of Louisiana to the United States, and 100 years later, it was the scene of the St. Louis World's Fair—the Louisiana Purchase Exposition. Today it is a transportation, manufacturing, and educational center.

Things to see in St. Louis: St. Louis Science Center, Missouri Historical Society, St. Louis Art Museum, St. Louis Zoological Park, Gateway Arch, Museum of Westward Expansion, Eads Bridge (1874), Riverboat *President*, Americana Emporium, Eugene Field House and Toy Museum (1845), St. Louis Sports Hall of Fame, National Bowling Hall of Fame, St. Louis Union Station, Missouri Botanical Garden, Jefferson Barracks Historical Park, Mercantile Money Museum, Purina Farms, Dog Museum, and Mastodon State Park.

Places to Visit

The National Park Service maintains six areas in the state of Missouri: Jefferson National Expansion Memorial, Ozark National Scenic Riverways, Wilson's

The Gateway Arch in St. Louis, a stainless-steel monument that stands 630-feet high, is the city's best known landmark.

Creek National Battlefield, George Washington Carver National Monument, Harry S. Truman National Historic Site, and Mark Twain National Forest. In addition, there are 40 state recreation areas.

Hannibal: Mark Twain Museum and Boyhood Home. The great writer lived here in the 1840s and 1850s.

Independence: The Harry S. Truman Library and Museum. One of the exhibits is a reproduction of Truman's White House office.

Lamar: Harry S. Truman Birthplace State Historic Site.

Lexington: Lafayette County Courthouse. Built in 1847, this is the oldest courthouse in constant use west of the Mississippi.

Monroe City: Mark Twain Birthplace and State Park. The park grounds include the two-room house where the author was born.

Osage Beach: Indian Burial Cave. A boat ride through an archeological cave.

St. Joseph: Jesse James Home. The cottage where the outlaw lived and was shot to death.

Sullivan: Meramec Caverns. These caverns were used as a Civil War gunpowder plant and a hideout by Jesse James in the 1870s.

Events

There are many events and organizations that schedule activities in the state of Missouri. Here are some of them.

Sports: American Royal Livestock, Horse Show, and Rodeo (Kansas City), Bootheel Rodeo (Sikeston).

Arts and Crafts: National Crafts Festival (Branson), Rose Week (Cape Girardeau), Columbia Art League Art Fair (Columbia), Prairie View Festival (St. Joseph), Watercolor USA (Springfield).

Music: Baldknobbers Hillbilly Jamboree (Branson), Lyric Opera (Kansas City), Kansas City Symphony (Kansas City), Kansas City Jazz Festival (Kansas City), State Ballet of Missouri (Kansas City), Opera Theatre of St. Louis (St. Louis), St. Louis Symphony (St. Louis), National Classic Jazz and Ragtime Festival (St. Louis), Muny Opera (St. Louis), Springfield Symphony (Springfield).

Entertainment: Riverfest (Cape Girardeau), Tom Sawyer Days (Hannibal), Truman Week Celebration (Independence), Ethnic Enrichment Festival (Kansas City), Battle of Lexington Reenactment (Lexington), Joseph Robidoux Festival (St. Joseph), Strassenfest (St. Louis), Hot Air Balloon Race (St. Louis), Missouri State Fair (Sedalia).

Tours: Walking Tour (Arrow Rock), Jour de Fête à Ste. Geneviève (Sainte Genevieve).

Theater: Old Mill Theater (Branson), Mark Twain Outdoor Theater (Hannibal), Molly Brown Dinner Theater (Hannibal), Missouri Repertory Theatre (Kansas City), Coterie Children's Theater (Kansas City), Starlight Theater (Kansas City), Repertory Theatre of St. Louis (St. Louis), Theatre Project Company (St. Louis), Tent Theater (Springfield).

Famous People

Many famous people were born in the state of Missouri. Here are a few:

Ed Asner b. 1929, Kansas City. Television actor: *The Mary Tyler Moore Show, Lou Grant*

Josephine Baker 1906-75, St. Louis. Dancer

Thomas Hart Benton 1889-1975, Neosho. Painter and muralist

Yogi Berra b. 1925, St. Louis. Hall of Fame baseball player

Bill Bradley b. 1943, Crystal City. Senate leader and basketball player

Omar N. Bradley 1893-1981, Clark. World War II general

Grace Bumbry b. 1937, St. Louis. Operatic mezzo-soprano

George Washington Carver 1861-1943, near Diamond Grove. Chemist

Walter Cronkite b. 1916, St. Joseph. Television news anchorman

Eugene Field 1850-95, St. Louis. Poet: "Little Boy Blue"

Dick Gregory b. 1932, St. Louis. Comedian, political activist, and nutritionist

Jean Harlow 1911-37, Kansas City. Film actress: *Hell's Angels, Saratoga*

Coleman Hawkins 1904-69, St. Joseph. Jazz saxophonist

Cal Hubbard 1900-77, Keytesville. Hall of Fame baseball umpire and Hall of Fame football player

Carl Hubbell 1903-88,

Modern-day Tom Sawyers' and Huck Finns' compete in a fence painting contest in Hannibal, Mark Twain's boyhood home.

Carthage. Hall of Fame baseball pitcher

Edwin P. Hubble 1889-1953, Marshfield. Astronomer

Langston Hughes 1902-67, Joplin. Poet: *The Weary Blues*

John Huston 1906-87, Nevada. Film director

Jesse James 1847-82, near

Centerville. Outlaw

Marianne Moore 1887-1972, Kirkwood. Pulitzer Prize-winning poet: *Collected Poems, Observations*

Geraldine Page 1924-87, Kirksville. Academy Award-winning actress: *The Trip to Bountiful*

J. C. Penney 1875-1971, Hamilton. Merchant

John J. Pershing 1860-1948, near Laclede. World War I general

Vincent Price b. 1911, St. Louis. Film actor: *Laura, Theatre of Blood*

Ginger Rogers b. 1911, Independence. Academy Award-winning actress: *Kitty Foyle, Top Hat*

Casey Stengel 1890-1975, Kansas City. Hall of Fame baseball manager

Sara Teasdale 1884-1933, St. Louis. Pulitzer Prize-winning poet: *Love Songs*

Calvin Trillin b. 1935, Kansas City. Newspaper columnist

Harry S. Truman 1884-1972,

Mark Twain's hometown of Hannibal was the setting for many of his writings.

Lamar. Thirty-third President of the United States

Mark Twain 1835-1910, Florida. Novelist: *Tom Sawyer*

Dick Van Dyke b. 1925, West Plains. Television actor: *The Dick Van Dyke Show*

Tom Watson b. 1949, Kansas City. Champion golfer

Earl Weaver b. 1930, St. Louis. Baseball manager

Roy Wilkins 1901-81, St. Louis. Civil rights leader

Colleges and Universities

There are many colleges and universities in Missouri. Here are the more prominent, with their locations, dates of founding, and enrollments.

Central Missouri State University, Warrensburg, 1871, 10,813

Lincoln University, Jefferson City, 1866, 3,063

Lindenwood College, St. Charles, 1827, 2,105

Maryville College-Saint Louis, St. Louis, 1872, 3,143

Missouri Southern State College, Joplin, 1937, 5,901

Missouri Western State College, St. Joseph, 1915, 4,338

Northeast Missouri State University, Kirksville, 1867, 6,158

Northwest Missouri State University, Maryville, 1905, 5,901

Rockhurst College, Kansas City, 1910, 3,239

Saint Louis University, St. Louis, 1818, 11,555

Southeast Missouri State University, Cape Girardeau, 1873, 8,520

Southwest Missouri State University, Springfield, 1906, 18,003

Stephens College, Columbia, 1833, 1,166

University of Missouri, Columbia, 1839, 24,220; Kansas City, 1933, 11,548; Rolla, 1870, 5,576; St. Louis, 1963, 12,872

Washington University, St. Louis, 1853, 9,415

Webster University, St. Louis, 1915, 9,061

William Jewell College, Liberty, 1849, 1,400

Where To Get More Information

Missouri Division of Tourism
Truman State Office Building
P.O. Box 1055
Jefferson City, MO 65102

Oklahoma

The state seal of Oklahoma, adopted in 1907, is circular. In the center is a five-pointed star, representing the Five Civilized Tribes of Indians that settled the territory. In the center of the star is the old territorial seal. The upper left point of the star contains the ancient seal of the Cherokee Nation; the top point, the seal of the Chickasaw Nation; the upper right point, the seal of the Choctaw Nation; the lower right point, the seal of the Seminole Nation; and the lower left point, the seal of the Creek Nation. Surrounding the star and between the points are 45 small stars, in groups of nine, representing the states already in the Union when Oklahoma entered as the 46th state. Around the edge of the seal is printed "Great Seal of the State of Oklahoma" and "1907," the year of the state's admission.

State Flag

Oklahoma's state flag is blue and contains a circular rawhide shield of an Indian warrior. On the shield are six crosses, and the bottom is fringed with seven eagle feathers. Placed upon the shield are an olive branch and an Indian peace pipe. Underneath is the word "Oklahoma." The flag was adopted in 1925.

State Salute to the Flag

In 1982, a salute to the state flag was selected: "I salute the flag of the State of Oklahoma. Its symbols of peace unite all people."

The view from atop Mount Scott in the Wichita Mountain National Wildlife Refuge in Lawton.

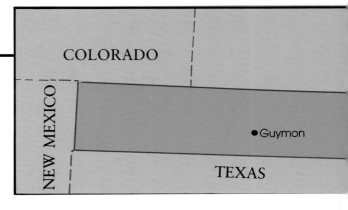

State Capital

The capital of Oklahoma was Guthrie from 1890 until 1910. Oklahoma City was named capital in 1910. The capitol building, based on Greek and Roman architecture, was completed in 1917. Constructed of Indiana limestone upon a granite base, it is ornamented with columns, and cost about $1.5 million. Oil wells surround the grounds.

State Name and Nicknames

The word Oklahoma comes from two Choctaw Indian words. *Okla* means "person," and *humma* means "red." Therefore, Oklahoma means "red person."

Oklahoma is called the *Sooner State* or *Boomer's Paradise*. Both of these refer to the opening of the territory in 1889. Sooners were those who illegally came into the territory to stake claims before the appointed hour. Boomers were those who came in legally to settle the new land.

The capitol building in Oklahoma City is one of the few statehouses in the country without a dome.

KANSAS

MISSOURI

ARKANSAS

TEXAS

OKLAHOMA

Miami

Alva

Blackwell

Bartlesville

Pawhuska

Vinita

Woodward

Enid

Pawnee

Pryor Creek

Perry

Claremore

Stillwater

Sand Springs

Tulsa

Cushing

Sapulpa

Broken Arrow

Guthrie

Tahlequah

Muskogee

BLACK KETTLE
NATIONAL
GRASSLANDS

Okmulgee

Salisaw

Elk City

★Oklahoma City

Henryetta

Canadian River

●Norman

Seminole

Anadarko

Wewoka

Hobart

Chickasha

Holdenville

OUACHITA
NATIONAL
FOREST

McAlester

Altus

Pauls Valley

Ada

Lawton

Duncan

Frederick

Ardmore

Red River

Durant

Hugo

Idabel

OUACHITA
NATIONAL
FOREST

N
△

★ State Capital
● Cities or towns
■ OF SPECIAL INTEREST

| 0 | 10 | 20 | | 40 | | 60 | | 80 | | 100 | Miles |

| 0 | 10 | 20 | 40 | 60 | 80 | 100 | 125 | 150 | Kilometres |

Mistletoe is the state flower.

State Flower
In 1893, mistletoe, *Phoradendron serotinum*, was adopted as state flower.

State Tree
Selected in 1937, the redbud tree, *Cercis canadensis*, is the state tree of Oklahoma.

State Bird
The scissortailed flycatcher, *Muscivora forticata*, was named state bird in 1951.

State Animal
The American buffalo, *Bison americanus*, was selected as state animal in 1972.

State Colors
Green and white have been the state colors since 1915.

State Fish
The white bass, *Morone chrysops*, was adopted as state fish in 1974.

State Grass
In 1972, Indian grass, *Sorghastrum nutans*, became the state grass.

The scissortailed flycatcher is the state bird.

State Poem
"Howdy Folks," by David Randolph Milsten, was selected in 1973.

State Reptile
Adopted in 1969, the collared lizard, *Crotophytus*, is the state reptile.

State Rock
Barite rose was named state rock in 1968.

State Songs
Oklahoma has had two state songs. From 1935 to 1953, it was "Oklahoma (A Toast)," by Harriet Parker Camden. In 1953, the present state song was substituted. It is "Oklahoma," with words by Oscar Hammerstein II and music by Richard Rodgers.

Population
The population of Oklahoma in 1990 was 3,157,604, making it the 28th most populous state. There are 45.2 persons per square mile—67.3 percent of the population live in towns and

cities. About 98 percent of all Oklahomans were born in the United States.

Geography and Climate

Bounded on the north by Colorado and Kansas, on the east by Missouri and Arkansas, on the south by Texas, and on the west by Texas and New Mexico, Oklahoma has an area of 69,919 square miles, making it the 18th largest state. The climate is temperate: humid in the south, colder in the north, humid in the east and central areas, and dry in the west.

In the west are high plains and in the east are mountains. In the central part are lowlands and plains. The highest point in the state, at 4,973 feet, is atop Black Mesa. The lowest point, at 289 feet, is along Little River in McCurtain County. The major waterways of Oklahoma are the Red, Arkansas, Blue, Kiamichi, Little, Mountain Fork, Washita, Canadian, Cimarron, Chikaskia, Illinois, Neosho (or Grand), Poteau, Salt Fork, and Verdigris rivers, and Cache Creek. Lake Eufaula is the largest lake.

Industries

The principal industries of the state of Oklahoma are mineral and energy exploration and production, printing and publishing, and agriculture. The chief manufactured products are nonelectrical machinery, fabricated metal products, and petroleum.

Agriculture

The chief crops of the state are wheat, hay, peanuts, grain sorghum, soybeans, corn, pecans, oats, barley, and rye. Oklahoma is also a livestock state, and there are estimated to be some 5.2 million cattle, 240,000 hogs and pigs, 136,000 sheep, and 4.65 million chickens and turkeys on its farms. Pine, oak, and hickory trees are harvested. Crushed stone, cement, sand, and gravel are important mineral resources.

Government

The governor is elected to a four-year term, as are the lieutenant governor, attorney general, treasurer, auditor, and superintendent of public instruction. The state legislature consists of a senate of 48 members and a house of representatives of 101 members. Senators serve four-year terms and representatives serve two-year terms. Each senator and representative is elected from a different district. The most recent state constitution was adopted in 1907. In addition to its two U.S. senators, Oklahoma has six representatives in the U.S. House of Representatives. The state has eight votes in the electoral college.

History

Before the Europeans arrived in what was to become Oklahoma, the area was populated by the Arapaho, Caddo, Cheyenne, Comanche, Kiowa, Osage, Pawnee, and Wichita Indians.

In 1541, the Spanish explorer Francisco Vásquez de Coronado came to the territory in search of gold. He was followed by another Spaniard, Hernando de Soto, that same year. Neither found gold, and both left the region.

Robert Cavelier, Sieur de la Salle, claimed all of the Mississippi River Valley for France in 1682. He named it Louisiana, after King Louis XIV. Although de la Salle never reached Oklahoma, it became part of that land claim. In 1762, France turned Louisiana over to Spain, but got it back in 1800. When the Louisiana Purchase was negotiated in 1803, Oklahoma became part of the United States. Oklahoma was first part of the District of Louisiana, then, in 1805, part of the Louisiana Territory. In 1812, it became part of the Missouri Territory, and, in 1819, part of the Arkansas Territory.

About 1819, the government began moving Indian tribes from other parts of the country into the region, which still had few non-Indian settlers. The main tribes that came were the Cherokee, Chickasaw, Choctaw, Creek, and Seminole—the Five Civilized Tribes. In 1824, the army built Fort Towson and Fort Gibson, and the five tribes were forced to move west.

After the Civil War, the government forced the five tribes to give up all their land because they had been slave holders and had supported the Confederacy. Much later, the authorities declared that the Indian Territory would be opened to settlement at noon on April 22, 1889. Thousands of eager settlers lined up on the border that day, waiting for a pistol shot that would open the territory. By evening, about 50,000 people had staked their claims. In 1890, the Territory of Oklahoma was established, and in 1907, Oklahoma became the 46th state in the Union.

During World War I, the state supplied agricultural and petroleum products to the armed forces. During the 1920s, more oil and gas deposits were discovered. The Great Depression of the 1930s hit the state hard. During World War II, farm products and oil became important again. Today, Oklahoma is still a major agricultural and industrial state, and has developed a booming tourist and recreational trade.

Sports

Sports, especially on the collegiate level, have always been important in Oklahoma. It, along with Iowa, is a wrestling hotbed. In basketball, Oklahoma A & M won the NCAA championship (1945, 1946). In football, Oklahoma A & M, Tulsa, and the University of Oklahoma have won numerous bowl games. The NCAA baseball championship has been won by the University of Oklahoma (1951) and Oklahoma State University (1959).

Major Cities

Oklahoma City (population 403,136). Founded in 1889, the capital city was empty prairie on the morning of April 22, 1889, the day of the great land rush. By sunset that day, its population was 10,000. Today it is an oil center, as well as a center of meat packing, grain milling, and cotton processing.

Things to see in Oklahoma City: State Capitol, State Museum of History, Oklahoma Art Center, ArtsPlace, International Photography Hall of Fame and Museum, Kirkpatrick Planetarium, OMNIPLEX, Harn Homestead and 1889er Museum, 45th Infantry Division Museum, National Softball Hall of Fame and Museum, National Cowboy Hall of Fame and Western Heritage Center, Oklahoma City Zoo, Aquaticus, Oklahoma Firefighters Museum, Oklahoma Museum of Art, Oklahoma Heritage Center, Oklahoma National Stock Yards, Frontier City, and White Water.

Tulsa (population 360,919). Founded in 1879, Tulsa was made by the oil industry. The first well came in in 1901. Today, it is still an oil center, but aviation and aerospace are important industries, and the city is a cultural and educational center.

Things to see in Tulsa: Thomas Gilcrease Institute of American History and Art, Tulsa County Historical Society Museum, Philbrook Museum of Art, Gershon and Rebecca Fenster Museum of Jewish Art, Tulsa Zoological Park, Tulsa Garden Center, Allen Ranch Inc., and Creek Nation Council Oak Tree.

Places to Visit

The National Park service maintains two areas in the state of Oklahoma: Chickasaw National Recreation Area and Ouachita National Forest. In addition, there are 39 state recreation areas.

Anadarko: Indian City—USA. Guided tours of reconstructed villages of seven Plains Indian tribes.

Claremore: Will Rogers Birthplace. The home where the great American humorist was born.

Durant: Fort Washita. Built in 1842, it was used to protect the Five Civilized tribes from the Plains Indians.

Oklahoma is a power in collegiate wrestling and the National Wrestling Hall of Fame in Stillwater is a place where the history of the sport is preserved.

Lawton: Fort Sill Military Reservation. There are 48 historic sites marked in this army installation.

Pawhuska: Osage Tribal Museum. The museum centering on Osage history.

Pawnee: Pawnee Bill Museum and Park. Memorabilia of the Wild West Show pioneer.

Ponca City: Pioneer Woman Museum. A pioneer home and ranch contain exhibits of pioneer family life.

Sallisaw: Sequoyah's Home. Built around 1829, this is the log cabin where the Cherokee who devised an Indian alphabet lived.

Stillwater: National Wrestling Hall of Fame. This museum is dedicated to wrestling history.

Tahlequah: Cherokee Heritage Center. Attractions include a museum and ancient village.

Events

There are many events and organizations that schedule activities of various kinds in the state of Oklahoma. Here are some of them.

Sports: Great Plains Stampede Rodeo (Altus), Durant Western Days and International Rodeo Association Rodeo (Durant), Rodeo of Champions (Elk City), National Parachute Championships (Muskogee), World Championship Quarter Horse Show (Oklahoma City), Creek Nation Rodeo and Festival (Okmulgee), Heart of America Bullriding Championship (Shawnee), International Finals Rodeo (Tulsa).

Arts and Crafts: Clinton Art Festival (Clinton), Festifall (Oklahoma City), Southwest Festival of the Arts (Weatherford).

Music: Tri-State Music Festival (Enid), Sanders Family Bluegrass Festival (McAlester), Oklahoma Philharmonic Orchestra (Oklahoma City), Ballet Oklahoma (Oklahoma City), Tulsa Ballet Theater (Tulsa), Tulsa Opera (Tulsa), Tulsa Philharmonic (Tulsa).

Entertainment: Kiowa Apache Ceremonial (Anadarko), American Indian Exposition (Anadarko), Santa Fe Trail Daze Celebration (Boise City), Kiamichi Owa Chito Festival (Broken Bow), Antique Car Swap Meet (Chickasha), Will Rogers Day Celebration (Claremore), Mid-America Summerfest (Enid), Cherokee Strip Celebration (Enid), Kiamichi Owa Chito Festival of the Forest (Idabel), Indian Summer Festival (Muskogee), 89er Celebration (Norman), Festival of the Arts (Oklahoma City), Red Earth (Oklahoma City), State Fair of Oklahoma (Oklahoma City), Osage Indian Tribal Dances (Pawhuska), Indian Powwow (Pawnee), Cherokee Strip Celebration (Perry), Ponca Indian Powwow (Ponca City), Sac and Fox Powwow (Shawnee), Cherokee National Holiday (Tahlequah), Tulsa Charity Horse Show (Tulsa), Tulsa Indian Powwow (Tulsa), Tulsa State Fair (Tulsa).

Tours: Dogwood Tours (Tahlequah).

Theater: The Oklahoma Shakespearean Festival (Durant), Rupel Jones Theater (Norman), Civic Center Music Hall (Oklahoma City), Lyric Theatre (Oklahoma City), "Trail of Tears" (Tahlequah).

Famous People

Many famous people were born in the state of Oklahoma. Here are a few:

Johnny Bench b. 1947, Oklahoma City. Hall of Fame baseball player

John Berryman 1914-72, McAlester. Pulitzer Prize-winning poet: *77 Dream Songs*

Gordon Cooper b. 1927, Shawnee. Astronaut

Ralph Ellison b. 1914, Oklahoma City. Novelist: *Invisible Man*

Paul Harvey b. 1918, Tulsa. Radio commentator

Van Heflin 1910-71, Walters. Academy Award-winning actor: *Johnny Eager, Shane*

Jeanne Kirkpatrick b. 1926, Duncan. U.S. ambassador to the United Nations

Mickey Mantle b. 1931, Spavinaw. Hall of Fame baseball player

Bill Moyers b. 1934, Hugo. Television commentator

James A. Pike 1913-69, Oklahoma City. Episcopal bishop

Will Rogers 1879-1935, near Oologah. Humorist

Willie Stargell b. 1940, Earlsboro. Hall of Fame baseball player

Jim Thorpe 1887-1953, Prague. Hall of Fame football player and Olympic gold medal winner

Gordon Cooper was the first American to spend a day in space when he orbited the earth 22 times on May 15, 1963.

Colleges and Universities

There are many colleges and universities in Oklahoma. Here are the more prominent, with their locations, dates of founding, and enrollments.

Central State University, Edmond, 1890, 14,214

Northeastern Oklahoma State University, Tahlequah, 1846, 8,723

Northwestern Oklahoma State University, Alva, 1897, 1,816

Oklahoma City University, Oklahoma City, 1911, 3,778

Oklahoma State University of Agriculture and Applied Science, Stillwater, 1890, 20,110

Oral Roberts University, Tulsa, 1963, 4,170

Southeastern Oklahoma State University, Durant, 1909, 3,714

Southwestern Oklahoma State University, Weatherford, 1901, 5,355

University of Oklahoma, Norman, 1890, 19,250

University of Tulsa, Tulsa, 1894, 4,318

Where To Get More Information

Oklahoma Tourism and Recreation Department Literature Distribution Center
P. O. Box 60000
Oklahoma City, OK 73146
Or Call 1-800-652-6552

Bibliography

General

Aylesworth, Thomas G. and Virginia L. Aylesworth, *Let's Discover the States: South Central*. New York: Chelsea House, 1988.

Arkansas

Ashmore, Harry S. *Arkansas: A History*. New York: Norton, 1984.

Bradley, Donald M. *Arkansas: Its Land and People*. Little Rock: Little Rock Museum of Science and Industry, 1980.

Carpenter, Allan. *Arkansas*, rev. ed. Chicago: Childrens Press, 1978.

Herndon, Dallas T. *Centennial History of Arkansas*. Easley, SC: Southern Historical Press, 1984.

Kansas

Carpenter, Allan. *Kansas*, rev. ed. Chicago: Childrens Press, 1981.

Davis, Kenneth S. *Kansas: A History*. New York: Norton, 1984.

Fradin, Dennis B. *Kansas in Words and Pictures*. Chicago: Childrens Press, 1981.

Richmond, Robert W. *Kansas: A Land of Contrasts*, 2nd ed. St. Louis: Forum Press, 1980.

Louisiana

Davis, Edwin A., and others. *Louisiana: The Pelican State*, rev. ed. Baton Rouge: Louisiana State University Press, 1985.

Fradin, Dennis B. *Louisiana in Words and Pictures*. Chicago: Childrens Press, 1981.

Taylor, Joe Gray. *Louisiana: A History*. New York: Norton, 1984.

Wall, Bennett H., and Charles E. O'Neill. *Louisiana: A History*. Arlington Heights, IL: Forum Press, 1984.

Missouri

Bailey, Bernadine. *Picture Book of Missouri*, rev. ed. Chicago: Whitman, 1974.

Carpenter, Allan. *Missouri*, rev. ed. Chicago: Childrens Press, 1974.

Fradin, Dennis B. *Missouri in Words and Pictures*. Chicago: Childrens Press, 1980.

Meyer, Duane G. *The Heritage of Missouri*, 3rd ed. St. Louis: River City Publishers, 1982.

Nagel, Paul C. *Missouri: A Bicentennial History*. New York: Norton, 1977.

Parrish, William E., and others. *Missouri: The Heart of the Nation*. St. Louis: Forum Press, 1980.

Oklahoma

Carpenter, Allan. *Oklahoma*, rev. ed. Chicago: Childrens Press, 1979.

Fradin, Dennis B. *Oklahoma in Words and Pictures*. Chicago: Childrens Press, 1981.

Gibson, Arrell M., and Victor E. Harlow. *The History of Oklahoma*. Norman, 1984.

Morgan, Howard W., and Anne H. *Oklahoma: A History*. New York: Norton, 1984.

A

Arapaho Indians, 21, 57
Arkansas Post, 12
Arkansas River, 10, 12, 21, 57
Atakapa Indians, 34
Atchafalaya River, 33

B

Barnett, Eva Ware, 10
Baton Rouge (LA), 31, *31*, 35, *35*
Battle of New Orleans, 34
Battle of Pea Ridge, 12
Bell Hall, *24*
Big Blue River, 21
Big Spring (MO), *41*
Black Mesa, 57
Black River, 33, 45
Blue River, 57
Boonville (MO), 46
Bowie, Jim, 9
Bradshaw, Terry, *37*
Buffalo National River, *7*

C

Cache Creek, 57
Caddo Indians, 11, 34, 57
Calcasieu River, 33
Camden, Harriet Parker, 56
Canadian River, 57
Cavelier, Robert, 12, 31, 34, 46, 58
Cherokee Indians, 58
Cheyenne Indians, 21, 57
Chickasaw Indians, 58
Chikaskia River, 57
Chitimacha Indians, 34
Choctaw Indians, 58
Cimarron River, 21, 57
Civil War, 20, 22, 34, 46, 58
Colleges and Universities (AR), 14; (KS), 26; (LA), 38; (MO), 50; (OK), 61
Comanche Indians, 21, 57
Cooper, Gordon, *61*
Creek Indians, 58
Crozat, Antoine, 34
Current River, 45

D

Davis, Jimmie H., 32
De Coronado, Francisco Vásquez, 21, 58
De Soto, Hernando, 11, 34, 58
Dexter (KS), 22

Donaldsonville (LA), 31
Driskill Mountain, 33
Dunklin County (MO), 45

E

Eppel, John Valentine, 44
Events: Arts and Crafts (AR), 13; (KS), 25; (LA), 37; (MO), 48; (OK), 60; Sports (AR), 24; (KS), 24; (LA), 36; (MO), 48; (OK), 60; Music (AR), 25; (KS), 25; (LA), 37; (MO), 48; (OK), 60; Entertainment (AR), 25; (KS), 25; (LA), 37; (MO), 48; (OK), 60; Tours (AR), 13; (LA), 37; (MO), 48; (OK), 60; Theater (AR), 13; (KS), 25; (LA), 37; (MO), 48; (OK), 60

F

Famous People (AR), 14; (KS), 25; (LA), 37; (MO), 48; (OK), 60
Fontane, Doralice, 32
Fort Gibson, 58
Fort Leavenworth (KS), 22, 24, *24*
Fort Smith, 12
Fort Towson, 58
Fox Indians, 46
French Quarter, *36*

G

Gasconade River, 45
Gateway Arch, *47*
Great Depression, 23
Gulf of Mexico, 33
Guthrie (OK), *54*
Gypsum (KS), *17*

H

Hammerstein, Oscar, 56
Hannibal (MO), 48, *49*
Higley, Dr. Brewster, 20

I

Illinois River, 57
Iron County (MO), 45

J

Jackson, Andrew, 34
Jackson, Claiborne F., 46
James River, 45
Jefferson City (MO), 43, *43*, 46
Jefferson, Thomas, *43*

Jennings (LA), 34
Jolliet, Louis, 11, 46

K

Kansa Indians, 9, 21
Kansas City (KS), 23
Kansas City (MO), 46, 47
Kansas City Chiefs, 46
Kansas City Royals, 46
Kansas River, 21
Kelly, Dan, 20
Kiamichi River, 57
King Louis XIV, 12, 31, 34, 46, 58
Kiowa Indians, 21, 57

L

Lake Eufaula, 57
Lake of the Ozarks, 45
Lake Pontchartrain, 33
Lawrence (KS), 22, *22*
Lawton (OK), *53*
Le Moyne, Jean Baptiste, 34
Lincoln, Abraham, 12, 46
Little Piney River, 45
Little River, 57
Little Rock (AR), 9, 12, *13*
Long, Huey P., *31*
Louisiana Purchase, 34, 46, 58

M

Magazine Mountain, 10
Marquette, Father Jacques, 9, 11, 46
Masters, Edgar Lee, *26*
McCurtain County (OK), 57
Memorial Stadium, *23*
Meramec River, 45
Middleton, Duff E., 20
Milford Lake, 21
Milsten, David Randolph, 56
Mississippi River, 10, 12, 33, 34, *35*, 45
Missouri Indians, 43
Missouri River, 21, 24, 43, 45, 46
Mitchell, Charles, 32
Monroe (LA), 34
Montgomery County (KS), 21
Mount Scott, *53*
Mount Sunflower, 21
Mountain Fork River, 57

N

Natchitoches, 34

National Wrestling Hall of Fame, *59*
Neosho River, 21, 57
New Orleans (LA), 31, 33, 34, 35, *36*
New Orleans Saints, 34

O

Oklahoma City (OK), 54, *54*, 59
Osage Indians, 11, 21, 46, 57
Ouachita River, 10, 33
Ozark National Forest, *11*

P

Pawnee Indians, 21, 57
Pearl River, 33
Pine Bluff, 13
Poteau River, 57

Q

Quapaw Indians, 11

R

Red River Valley, 33
Red River, 10, 33, 57
Republican River, 21
Revolutionary War, 34
Robinson, Brooks, *14*
Rodgers, Richard, 56

S

Sabine River, 33
Saint Joseph (MO), *45*
Saline River, 21
Salt Fork River, 57
Sauk Indians, 46
Seminole Indians, 58
Shannon, J. R., 44

Smoky Hill River, 21
Solomon River, 21
St. Charles (MO), 43
St. Francis River, 45
St. Francis, 10
St. Louis (MO), 46, 47, *47*
St. Louis Blues, 46
St. Louis Cardinals, 46
State Animal (KS), 20; (OK), 56
State Banner (KS), 17
State Beverage (AR), 10; (LA), 32
State Bird (AR), 10, (KS), 20, *20*; (LA), 32, *32*; (MO), 44, *44*; (OK), 56, *56*
State Capital (AR), 9, *9*; (KS), 18, *18*; (LA), 31, *31*; (MO), 43, *43*; (OK), 54, *54*
State Colors (OK), 56
State Crustacean (LA), 32
State Dog (LA), 32
State Fish (OK), 56
State Flag (AR), 7, *7*; (KS), 17, *17*; (LA), 29, *29*; (MO), 41, *41*; (OK), 53, *53*
State Flower (AR), 10, *10*; (KS), 20, *20*; (LA), 32, *32*; (MO), 44, *44*; (OK), 56, *56*
State Fossil (LA), 32; (MO), 44
State Fruit (LA), 32
State Gem (AR), 10; (LA), 32
State Grass (OK), 56
State Insect (AR), 10; (KS), 20; (LA), 32; (MO), 44
State March, (KS), 20
State Mineral (AR), 10; (MO), 44
State Motto (AR), 7; (KS), 17; (LA), 29; (MO), 41
State Musical Instrument (AR), 10; (MO), 44
State Name and Nicknames (AR), 9; (KS), 20; (LA), 31; (MO), 43; (OK), 54
State Poem (OK), 56
State Reptile (LA), 32; (OK), 56

State Rock (AR), 10; (MO), 44; (OK), 56
State Salute to the Flag (OK), 53
State Seal (AR), 5, *5*; (KS), 15, *15*; (LA), 27, *27*; (MO), 39, *39*; (OK), 51, *51*
State Song (AR), 10; (KS), 20; (LA), 32; (MO), 44; (OK), 56
State Tree (AR), 10; (KS), 20; (LA), 32; (MO), 44; (OK), 56
State Tree Nut (MO), 44
Ste. Genevieve, 46
Stillwater (OK), *59*, 60

T

Taum Sauk Mountain, 45
Topeka (KS), *18*, 23
Tulsa (OK), 59
Tunica Indians, 34
Twain, Mark, 48, *49, 50*

U

University of Kansas, *23*

V

Van Buren (MO), *41*
Verdigris River, 21, 57

W

War of 1812, 34, 46
Washita River, 57
White Castle (LA), 34
White River, 10, 45
Wichita (KS), 23
Wichita Indians, 21, 57
World War I, 23, 46, 58
World War II, 12, 34, 46, 58

Photo Credits/Acknowledgments

Photos on pages 3 (top), 5-7, 9-11, 13, courtesy Arkansas Department of Parks and Tourism; pages 6-7, 9, 11, 13, courtesy A. C. Haralson; pages 16-18, 20-21, 23, courtesy Kansas Department of Economic Development; pages 28-29, 30-33, 35-36, courtesy Louisiana Office of Tourism; pages 4 (top), 39-41, 43-45, 47, 49, Missouri Division of Tourism; pages 52-54, 56, 59, courtesy Oklahoma Division of Tourism/Fred W. Marvel; pages 3 (middle) and 15, courtesy Kansas Secretary of State; pages 3 (bottom) and 27, courtesy Louisiana Secretary of State; pages 4 (bottom) and 51, courtesy Oklahoma Secretary of State; page 14 courtesy TV Sports Mailbag; pages 22, 26, 50, courtesy New York Public Library; page 24 courtesy Fort Leavenworth; page 37 courtesy Pittsburgh Steelers; page 61 courtesy NASA.

Cover photograph courtesy Arkansas Department of Parks and Tourism